CEREAL
CITY GUIDE
NEW YORK

ABRAMS IMAGE,
NEW YORK

A City Guide by C E R E A L

Rosa Park, Editor in Chief
Rich Stapleton, Creative Director
Richard Aslan, Subeditor
Studio Faculty, Book Design

Photography by
Alice Gao, Cerruti Draime, Justin Chung,
Matthew Johnson, Rosa Park, Samantha
Goh, Sharon Radisch

Words by
Jenny Bahn, John Pawson, Kris Seto,
Leigh Patterson, Libby Borton, Lucy
Brook, Matthew Johnson, Rosa Park

Editor: Laura Dozier
Design Manager: Danny Maloney
Production Manager: Katie Gaffney

Library of Congress Control Number:
2017956799

ISBN: 978-1-4197-3285-0
eISBN: 978-1-68335-339-3

Printed and bound in China
10 9 8 7 6 5

Abrams books are available at special discounts when purchased
in quantity for premiums and promotions as well as fundraising
or educational use. Special editions can also be created to
specification. For details, contact specialsales@abramsbooks.com
or the address below.

ABRAMS The Art of Books
195 Broadway, New York, NY 10007
abramsbooks.com

THE CONCEPT

We, at Cereal, have traveled to cities around the world and sought out places we believe to be unique, interesting, and enjoyable. Our aim is to produce guides that would befit Cereal readers and modern travelers alike, recommending a tightly edited selection of experiences that combine quality with meticulous design. If the food is top-notch, so too is the space that accompanies it. You'll soon notice that our version of the perfect trip is woven in with an understated flair and a penchant for grand landscapes, both natural and constructed. Within these pages, you will find the practical advice you need on where to stay, where to eat, what to see, and where to shop.

THE GUIDE

This guide to New York City features a considered selection of shops, hotels, restaurants, cafés, and points of interest. Not intending to be comprehensive, we present a discerning edit of our favorite places to visit in the city.

All photographs, copy, and illustrations are original and exclusive to Cereal.

CONTENTS

A City Guide by CEREAL

PLACES TO VISIT

INTERVIEWS

ESSAYS

ADDITIONAL INFORMATION

NEW YORK

Scott Fitzgerald found "wild promise of all the mystery and beauty in the world" here. Angela Carter believed "cities have sexes: London is a man, Paris is a woman, and New York is a well-adjusted transsexual." Simone de Beauvoir confided "there is something in the New York air that makes sleep useless." Words are never enough for this city, so often evoked that even a first visit entails almost constant déjà vu. This quintessential urban jungle delights us and tests us in equal measure. "In New York," as Charles Bukowski reminded us, "you've got to have all the luck."

COUNTRY	USA
AIRPORT	JFK / LGA
LANGUAGE	ENGLISH
CURRENCY	USD
DIALING CODE	+1

A PHOTO ESSAY

photos by MATTHEW JOHNSON

NEIGHBORHOODS

MAP
of NEW YORK CITY

34

35

45

33

31

29

32

44

30

27

28

43

24

25

26

23

18

22

41

19   20   21

42

17

13   14   15   16

10

7   8   11   12

9

3   5   39   40

6

4   38

37

1   2   36

N

1:230,000 SCALE

PLACES TO VISIT

THE GREENWICH HOTEL

HOTEL
in TRIBECA

Close to the heart of Tribeca is the resplendent Greenwich Hotel, hewn in the classic New York style of wrought iron and redbrick. Swathed in rich velvet and accented with dark wood, its unique rooms sigh with timeless sophistication and charm. Outside, foliage cascades over the rolling arches of the tranquil courtyard. Perched atop the hotel is the *wabi*-inspired Tribeca penthouse, created by Axel Vervoordt and Tatsuro Miki, wreathed with a crown of winding wisteria.

+1 212-941-8900
thegreenwichhotel.com

377 Greenwich Street
New York, NY 10013

PUBLIC

HOTEL
on the LOWER EAST SIDE

Designed by prizewinning architects Herzog & de Meuron, PUBLIC is Ian Schrager's affordable redefinition of a luxury hotel. The mellow glow of plywood and smooth concrete distills a sense of ease and *lagom*—meaning "just enough" in Swedish. Beds are embraced by seemingly free-floating booths in smaller rooms, while larger suites allow the space to drink in the cityscape through floor-to-ceiling windows. Spend time in the eclectic store, the shapeshifting performance space, and especially the rooftop bar.

+1 212-735-6000
publichotels.com

215 Chrystie Street
New York, NY 10002

11 HOWARD

HOTEL

in SOHO

Upon entering 11 Howard, you are greeted by a black Alexander Calder mobile hanging amid a serene color palette of warm beiges and cool grays. From here, you can turn left toward the on-site French restaurant, Le Coucou, or head up the spiral staircase to The Library—a communal space where you can eat, drink, work, and relax—and The Blond, the hotel lounge. Each of the property's 221 rooms comes with light oak floors and handcrafted furnishings that pay homage to Danish minimalism and an effortlessly cool New York style. And if you're hankering after interior items of a similar vein, you can wander down to the ground floor to Studio Oliver Gustav, a gallery and design studio from Copenhagen, to browse their wares. Donating a portion of its revenues to the Global Poverty Project, 11 Howard is a hub for the creative and the conscious.

+1 212-235-1111
11howard.com

11 Howard Street
New York, NY 10013

1 HOTEL BROOKLYN BRIDGE

HOTEL
in DUMBO

+1 877-803-1111
1hotels.com

60 Furman Street
Brooklyn, NY 11201

Planted on the edge of Brooklyn Bridge Park, 1 Hotel Brooklyn Bridge is a homegrown haven, offering breathing space for the weary traveler. Inspired by sustainability and green living, it weaves a portrait of Brooklyn's thriving community and collective consciousness toward the environment from a resident's perspective, ranging from artworks narrating the borough's storied past to locally sourced treats at the all-day café. With serene, unspoiled views of the East River and Manhattan skyline, you can tend to your well-being among fresh greenery, repurposed materials imbued with history, and lampshades grown (yes, grown) from mushrooms by Danielle Trofe. Each room even has its own yoga mat.

THE CARLYLE

There's no better welcome to New York City than The Carlyle's unfurling stars and stripes above a golden doorway. Built in the Art Deco style in 1930, its sophistication and elegance has drawn cultural icons from Frank Sinatra and Marilyn Monroe to JFK. Jazz music swims from Bemelmans Bar, where renowned musicians play, including Woody Allen and the Eddy Davis New Orleans Jazz Band. Just a stone's throw from Central Park and Museum Mile, The Carlyle offers a true taste of New York glamour.

+1 212-744-1600
rosewoodhotels.com/en/the-carlyle-new-york

35 East 76th Street
New York, NY 10021

TÉ COMPANY

CAFÉ
in the WEST VILLAGE

The humble Té Company is a purveyor of fine
Taiwanese teas, providing premium oolong
tea to revive, soothe, and embolden your soul.
Steeped in history and mythology, each blend
has a beautiful name, such as Buddha Hand,
Crimson Grace, Blossom Dearie, and Iron
Goddess. Tea is served with little cakes and
small dishes, but be aware—reservations are
not taken. If you can't stop for too long, at least
pick up a pack of their famous fresh-baked
pineapple *linzers* to enjoy at home.

+1 929-335-3168
te-nyc.com

163 West 10th Street
New York, NY 10014

LA MERCERIE

CAFÉ
in SOHO

Inside home décor emporium Roman and Williams Guild in SoHo, La Mercerie is a laid-back but sumptuous café, which serves contemporary French cuisine by Parisian chef Marie-Aude Rose. In the morning, buttery croissants and brioche tumble from the pastry counter, and soft-boiled eggs topped with breadcrumbs, cauliflower, tofu purée, and parmesan shavings fly out of the kitchen. The all-day menu, paired with a French wine list, includes filet steaks in cognac sauce, oysters in seaweed butter, *pommes dauphine* with blue cheese, and crispy grilled buckwheat crêpes. With an excellently crafted cocktail menu to boot, La Mercerie is as refined a café as they come.

+1 212-852-9097
lamerceriecafe.com

53 Howard Street,
New York, NY 10013

LA MERCERIE CAFÉ

RUSS & DAUGHTERS CAFÉ

For over a century, the Russ & Daughters store has been ingrained in the fabric of New York City as a grocery haven for Jewish immigrants, offering herring and matzo, capers and whitefish. Russ & Daughters Café continues the authenticity of that culinary heritage, but with aesthetics that blend in a little more with its hip Lower East Side contemporaries. Grab a classic bagel board with lox and schmear, or a traditional knish, or splurge on some of the best caviar in the city. If you're keen on getting a table, we recommend arriving soon after opening time.

+1 212-475-4880
russanddaughterscafe.com

127 Orchard Street
New York, NY 10002

OKONOMI

In the soft gray space of Okonomi, *ichiju sansai* is served. Literally meaning "one soup, three dishes," this traditional Japanese set meal consists of rice, soup, fish, and pickles. The Okonomi version comes with seven-grain rice, miso soup, and fresh vegetables. Everything is blanched, torched, or roasted, without butter or oil, and plated on tableware made from New York soil, water, and wood, handcrafted by Jordan Colón. The flavors are pure, unadulterated joy. Reflecting the principles of balance and nutrition, *ichiju sansai* is the antithesis of indulgence; it is necessity.

okonomibk.com/home

150 Ainslie Street
Brooklyn, NY 11211

DIMES

There is a comfort food rule of thumb: Eating out of a bowl makes everything taste better. Given how addictive the food at Dimes is, there must be some truth to it. This easygoing eatery focuses on health-conscious, earthy California-style cuisine. Picture simple superfood ingredients—such as kale, coconut milk, beets, brussels sprouts, quinoa, acai, and salmon—combined in imaginative, unexpected ways and bursting with flavor.

+1 212-925-1300
dimesnyc.com

49 Canal Street
New York, NY 10002

FIVE LEAVES

RESTAURANT
in GREENPOINT

Travel to the Greenpoint side of McCarren Park on any given weekend, and you are likely to find a small gathering of salivating brunchers waiting their turn to sink their teeth into the incredible offerings at this chill Aussie-influenced New American bistro. Try the signature burger, truffle fries, or ricotta pancakes. Equally appetizing is the vintage nautical decor.

+1 718-383-5345
fiveleavesny.com

18 Bedford Avenue
Brooklyn, NY 11222

FIVE LEAVES RESTAURANT

BIRDS OF A FEATHER

RESTAURANT
in WILLIAMSBURG

Head to Birds of a Feather for lively twists on traditional Sichuan cuisine. The menu pairs the typical zingy spice of Sichuan pepper with more delicately balanced, aromatic dishes. Dim sum is a noteworthy specialty, particularly the crab soup buns served in a bamboo steamer, while other stand-out entrees include crispy fried egg plants, poached wontons in chilli sauce, and okra wrapped in thin slices of pork. Share as many plates as you can, you will want to try everything.

+1 718-969-6800
birdsofafeatherny.com

191 Grand Street
Brooklyn, NY 11211

LILIA

RESTAURANT
in WILLIAMSBURG

Relish in the warm embrace of Lilia. Once an automotive body shop, it has blossomed into a blissful sanctuary of Italian delights under the careful, nurturing eye of chef Missy Robbins. In the morning, the café counter is draped with bite-size *fritelle di san Guiseppe*, *maritozzi*, and *bomboloni*, and the space is awash with the aroma of brewing coffee. By evening, an orange glow, reminiscent of a Negroni at sunset, descends. As handmade ribbons of rich golden pasta swirl on forks, laughter and chatter ripple through the scent of wood-fired seafood.

+1 718-576-3095
lilianewyork.com

567 Union Avenue
Brooklyn, NY 11222

EN JAPANESE BRASSERIE

Amid the many upscale Japanese establishments in the West Village, EN Japanese Brasserie stands out thanks to its striking interior, *izakaya* spirit, and seasonal cuisine honoring the flavor of every ingredient. Sake and *shochu* lovers will rejoice in the extensive selection. Be sure to order the house-made tofu—a must-eat treat.

+1 212-647-9196
enjb.com

435 Hudson Street
New York, NY 10014

ESTELA

RESTAURANT
in NOLITA

If you find yourself shopping in the many beautiful stores in Soho and Nolita, take a break like a seasoned New Yorker at Estela. Whether it's for brunch, dinner, or a cocktail, Estela offers a cozy reprieve slightly removed from its bustling neighborhood. Get the *burrata* or the ricotta dumplings, and hang out for a while.

+1 212-219-7693
estelanyc.com

47 East Houston Street
New York, NY 10012

MAIALINO

Located in the Gramercy Park Hotel, Maialino is one of our favorite spots in the city. This warm and inviting restaurant evokes a Roman *trattoria*, with a standing barista station, a sweets and pastry front, and a lively bar, each of which breathes a unique energy into the space. Executive chef Nick Anderer serves a rustic Italian menu that's top-notch. You can't go wrong with anything on the menu, but the ricotta pancakes with peach jam hold a sweet spot in our hearts (and bellies).

+1 212-777-2410
maialinonyc.com

2 Lexington Avenue
New York, NY 10010

MAIALINO RESTAURANT

FLORA BAR

RESTAURANT
on the UPPER EAST SIDE

+1 646-558-5383
florabarnyc.com

The Met Breuer, 945 Madison Avenue
New York, NY 10021

Housed beneath The Met Breuer art museum, Flora Bar, swathed in concrete and black leather, has an unabashedly brutalist aesthetic. The restaurant is open all day, and long after the museum has closed. Chef Ignacio Mattos invites you to share his love of seafood, from clams to lobster, with playful flavor combinations and textures. So have a drink or two at the long bar, or take a seat for dinner. It's the perfect place to soak in the artistic splendor of the floors above.

MORGENSTERN'S FINEST ICE CREAM

ICE CREAM SHOP
in the BOWERY

Don't expect to be the only one lining up for Morgenstern's unique flavors, but don't let the line deter you, either. The offerings on a special menu rotate among different acclaimed chefs' aspirational desserts, while the in-house menu provides mainstays such as burnt honey vanilla and coconut ash. Maybe you'll be lucky and find yourself in town during Kanye West's ice cream week for a "Beautiful Morning" milkshake (coffee ice cream and cornflakes).

+1 212-209-7684
morgensternsnyc.com

2 Rivington Street
New York, NY 10002

Morgenstern's
FINEST ICE CREAM

DRINKS

HAND-PACKED PINT	$13
PRE-PACKED PINT	$11

HOUSE SODAS	$2.5
FLOATS	$8
SHAKES	$9/12
COOLERS	$8
AFFOGATOS	$6.5

TOPPINGS

CARAMEL	PICOSOS PEANUTS
SALTED CARAMEL	ALEPPO PECANS
SESAME CARAMEL	PISTACHIOS
FUDGE	TOASTED ALMONDS
HONEY	WALNUTS
WHIPPED CREAM	BLACK WALNUTS
CHOCOLATE SHOTS	SESAME HONEYCOMB
CHOCOLATE CHUNKS	CASHEWS
PRETZELS	HONEYED CASHEWS
PICKLED PINEAPPLE	JUNIOR MINTS
LUXARDO CHERRIES	LEMON JAM
TOASTED COCONUT	CONDENSED MILK

ALL TOPPINGS .50 EACH

KIDS'

CONE/CUP	4
MINI MORGENSTERN	7.5
BUTTERSCOTCH BANGER	6.5
LITTLE LION HEARTED	6.5

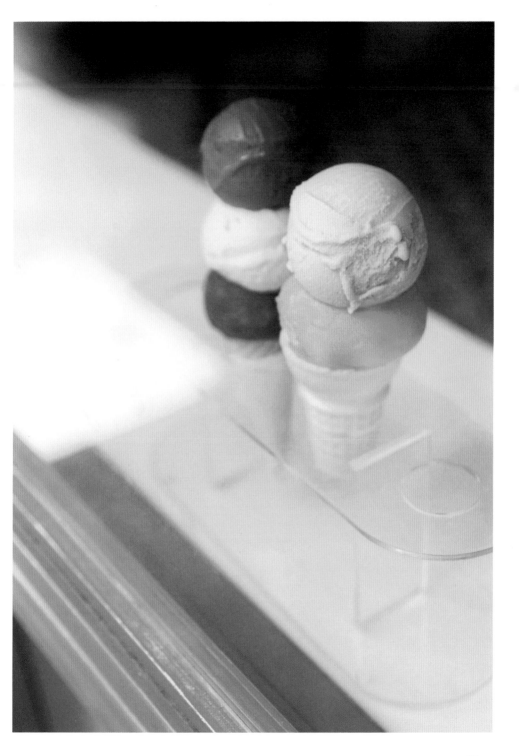

BAR PISELLINO

Bar Pisellino is an all-day Italian bar, modelled after the classic cafes of Venice, Rome and Florence. Every detail is attended to, from the oak-panelled interior to the ornate napkins placed under each drink. It occupies a narrow corner space directly opposite sister restaurant Via Carota, making it an excellent aperitif stop while you wait for a table across the street. Stop by in the morning for an espresso and bomoblone at the marble-topped bar, return in the afternoon for a leisurely Aperol spritz and a tramezzino outside, and meet friends in the evening for classic Italian cocktails.

barpisellino.com

52 Grove Street
New York, NY 10014

ANTHOM

ANTHOM specializes in thoughtful, contemporary women's clothing, inspired by the model of a curious, intelligent, and discerning woman. The rails in this gallery-like setting also carry partner brand Yune Ho alongside a diverse collection of designers, including Marni, Rejina Pyo, and J. Hannah. The knowledgeable staff are always happy to assist, whether advising on a single piece of jewelry or creating an entire look. With its emphasis on functional beauty, responsibility, and positivity, ANTHOM is the complete style experience.

+1 877-747-1776
shopanthom.com

25 Mercer Street
New York, NY 10013

LA GARÇONNE

This elegant online retailer has moved into a brick-and-mortar home in Tribeca: a Japanese-inspired, white-walled space to fit their minimalist aesthetic. Shop for the best in luxurious, understated womenswear and lifestyle brands, including The Row, Maison Margiela, La Garçonne Moderne, and J.W. Anderson.

+1 646-553-3303
lagarconne.com

465 Greenwich Street
New York, NY 10013

SHW

Part gift shop, part home shop, and full of hidden wonders, SHW is a small boutique located in the East Village that stocks a variety of charming, just-offbeat-enough tchotchkes, including geometric jewelry, statement vases, handmade cards, Japanese ceramics, and tabletop decor. Shop owner Urte Tylaite curates a diverse collection of treasures from local and international artists. Leave plenty of time to explore every corner.

+1 212-539-0200
shwjewelry.com

307 East 9th Street
New York, NY 10003

C'H'C'M'

APPAREL SHOP
in NOHO

+1 646-820-9243
chcmshop.com

2 Bond Street
New York, NY 10012

Sweetu Patel has created a temple to true modern menswear at this Noho boutique. The shop carries its namesake brand alongside special collaboration projects and a changing roster of select, easy-to-wear but hard-to-find international labels. There's a purity to every garment—a weightiness that can be seen in the cut, materials, and impeccable detailing. Drop in regularly to catch the rotating artwork, events, and pop-up shop additions.

C'H'C'M' APPAREL SHOP

SAVE KHAKI UNITED

Seek simple and classic style at Save Khaki United. With reputable hard-wearing and long-lasting clothes for men, they create everyday essentials in earthy and cool tones. Explore their comfortable and practical workwear range in high-quality fabrics, including cotton and cashmere—the staples of the brand—from flannel shirts to simple chinos. They have two stores in New York (photographs are of the Lafayette location), both fully stocked with classic-cut clothes and other must-have lifestyle items.

+1 212-925-0130
savekhaki.com

317 Lafayette Street
New York, NY 10012

NALATA NALATA

There's something poetic about holding an object that has been designed and crafted to the point of perfection. You can feel the painstaking care, thought, and discipline that have been poured into it. At Nalata Nalata, you can also learn about its history. With a focus on the artists, and on how each item is made, store owners Stevenson Aung and Angélique Chmielewski have assembled a collection of their favorite functional objects from around the world. Expect exceptional items for living, lounging, storing, cooking, and more.

+1 212-228-1030
nalatanalata.com

2 Extra Place
New York, NY 10003

192 BOOKS

192 Books is reliably free from fodder, only stocking fiction, art books, and children's literature with "lasting interest" for the well-read and the curious. They host regular readings and events, including a children's story hour on Wednesdays. For the adults, guests have included distinguished writers such as Chimamanda Ngozi Adichie, Martin Amis, Julian Barnes, Salman Rushdie, and Zadie Smith. With amenable staff and a relaxed atmosphere, it's worth a pilgrimage to peruse their shelves.

+1 212-255-4022
192books.com

192 10th Avenue
New York, NY 10011

192 BOOKS BOOKSHOP

McNALLY JACKSON

BOOKSHOP
in WILLIAMSBURG

Stumble into Sarah McNally's two-story bookshop and you may never leave. Located inside the converted Lewis Steel Building, the independent icon has a comprehensive selection of books and magazines, all organized by geographical region. Their well-read staff can help you find exactly what you're looking for, or unearth something entirely novel. Check the calendar for author readings or workshops taking place during your visit. For a beautifully curated range of stationery and other items for the office, visit McNally Jackson's sister shop in Nolita, Goods for the Study.

+1 718-387-0115
mcnallyjackson.com

76 North 4th Street, Unit G
Brooklyn, NY 11249

DASHWOOD BOOKS

Where do the world's most influential photographers and creatives go to find inspiration? This Bond Street basement shop is a dedicated homage to the image and image makers, specializing in rare and out-of-print photography books. You can find independently published gems that cover preeminent photographers and their work from the 1950s to the present day.

+1 212-387-8520
dashwoodbooks.com

33 Bond Street
New York, NY 10012

THE MORGAN LIBRARY & MUSEUM

Tucked into Manhattan's Murray Hill neighborhood, this literature-lover's oasis was originally founded in 1906 to house the private library of financier J.P. Morgan. The museum is filled with rich relics, original manuscripts, rare prints, medieval artworks, and historical drawings from Leonardo da Vinci, Michelangelo, Raphael, and Rembrandt. View J.D. Salinger's letters, soak in Edgar Allan Poe's phantasmagorical world, and admire the three ancient Gutenberg Bibles in this beautiful Palladian space.

+1 212-685-0008
themorgan.org

225 Madison Avenue
New York, NY 10016

The East Room:
The Library.

Room overview

THE NOGUCHI MUSEUM

MUSEUM
in ASTORIA

An overwhelming sense of peace descends whenever you enter The Noguchi Museum. The immaculate space, designed by the influential artist and sculptor himself, showcases a wide range of his work, including monumental stone sculptures, landscape architecture, furniture design, and photography. It's the embodiment of Noguchi's philosophy: a focus on surface, space, and the utmost respect for his materials.

+1 718-204-7088
noguchi.org

9-01 33rd Road
Long Island City, NY 11106

NEW YORK PUBLIC LIBRARY

ADDITIONAL
RECOMMENDATIONS

THE BEEKMAN   *Hotel | thebeekman.com*

THE WILLIAM VALE   *Hotel | thewilliamvale.com*

MADAME VO   *Restaurant | madamevo.com*

RUBY'S CAFÉ   *Restaurant | rubyscafe.com*

HUDSON CLEARWATER   *Restaurant | hudsonclearwater.com*

ABCV   *Restaurant | abchome.com/dine/abcv*

BESSOU   *Restaurant | bessou.nyc*

DAILY PROVISIONS   *Bakery & Café | dailyprovisionsnyc.com*

SEL RROSE   *Bar | selrrose.com*

OROBORO   *Womenswear Shop | oroboro.com*

THE FRANKIE SHOP   *Apparel & Accessories Shop | thefrankieshop.com*

KETTL   *Tea Shop | kettl.co*

THE PRIMARY ESSENTIALS   *Lifestyle Shop | theprimaryessentials.com*

MUSEUM OF MODERN ART   *Museum | moma.org*

NEW YORK PUBLIC LIBRARY   *Library | nypl.org*

SOLOMON R. GUGGENHEIM MUSEUM   *Museum | guggenheim.org*

ABCV

UNIS

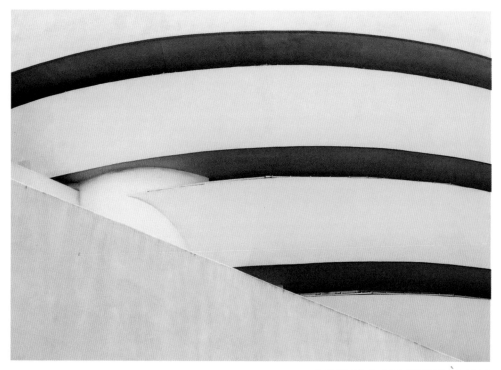

SOLOMON R. GUGGENHEIM MUSEUM

INTERVIEWS

A CITY OF ONE'S OWN:
AN INTERVIEW WITH PHILLIP LIM

words by JENNY BAHN
portraits by MATTHEW JOHNSON
Interiors photography by CERRUTI DRAIME

It has been fourteen years since Phillip Lim arrived in New York City with two suitcases and the spent portion of a one-way ticket in his hand. He still doesn't feel like a New Yorker. He hopes he never does. Because, to Lim, to force a name upon the feeling of living here, of being of this place, is an exchange threatened by a romantic superstition: the day he becomes a New Yorker, he fears the spell will be broken, the love affair over. And Phillip Lim very much wishes to remain in love with New York.

As a child in Huntington Beach, California, Lim did not grow up wistfully dreaming of parts further east. He was preoccupied with his hometown's surf and skate culture. He was grateful for warm air and blue skies, thankful for his proximity to the beach; a West Coast kid, through and through. But then, he moved to New York City, not as a naive and wide-eyed twenty-something, but as a 30-year-old adult on the precipice of an unseen greatness. The following year, at age 31, this pivotal number became a cypher in the brand he launched that year, 3.1 Phillip Lim. It would serve as a permanent reminder of the uniquely transformational power New York City offers those daring enough to risk its embrace.

"You have to be a little brave or a little crazy to come to New York with just a dream," Lim says. "But that's what people do." The designer, in his own act of gallantry or lunacy, began fashioning a life for himself here, placing roots. He found his first home, a second-floor apartment in an old Chelsea brownstone. There was a terrace outside his bedroom. "I wanted something quintessentially

New York," he explains, "to make living here feel more real." He stayed. He made friends, built a business. He got a pet, a white French bulldog named Oliver. New York got its hooks into him. "I fell in love," says Lim. "I still am."

Sustainable affection, it is said, requires a loose and judicious grip. Lim allows himself to entertain the idea of a different life in a different place, but he never gets far. "I was just in Shanghai," he confesses. "I love many cities in Asia and I think I could be happy living there, but even as I was telling my friend that same thing, I was already backtracking, saying, 'But it's not New York.' Because nothing is." He praises the city's unrivaled diversity, its energy and possibility. He laments the constant construction, the filth, the incessant honking of horns, and the high price paid to endure it all. Lim knows, though, you cannot have one without the other. Here, the good is inexorably bound to the bad.

To know New York is to know the agonizing despair that is loving it. Desperately, begrudgingly, faithfully. Few cities in the world instill such conflicted passion. "It can be gritty and lonely," Lim admits. "The summers are too hot and the winters are too cold. It almost hurts you. But, if you love it, you can't get enough of that pain." In exchange for these discomforts, New York City proffers the sweetest rewards. "It has given me my business, my closest friends," Lim tells me. "It has kept me company by giving me places to explore when I've felt anxious or alone. I have eaten in diners at 3 a.m. I've walked across the Brooklyn Bridge at sunset. I have seen it change."

Lim, too, has changed. His former selves live on, joining the specters of innumerable others on streets forever in flux. "Every scratched subway seat, every dirty slice of pavement or dusty park bench tells a million stories. And your story, your history is everywhere. I see my younger self standing on street corners in Chinatown, cutting across Houston Street, running up the steps to old apartments, old neighborhoods, with old friends. It is a very nostalgic city, very haunted in some ways. But also a city of reincarnation and possibility and promise. That is why you stay, why you love it."

Today, Lim lives in a SoHo loft filled with beautiful objects, prizes for a hard-won success born in and of this place. Altered as his life has become since he first arrived, Lim remains as enchanted with New York City as ever. He does not tire of the push and pull, its charms and its horrors. He continues to find inspiration in the everyday moments it presents, in the wants and fears of its striving inhabitants. His favorite time of day, though, is late at night, when the crowds dissipate and the sidewalks empty. When all that is left is the steam and the cobblestones and the feeling, however brief, that the city is his own.

———

31PHILLIPLIM.COM

THE FOUR HORSEMEN:
AN INTERVIEW WITH RANDY MOON &
JUSTIN CHEARNO

words by LEIGH PATTERSON
photos by CERRUTI DRAIME

Like all great things in New York City, The Four Horsemen in Williamsburg is the result of the careful splicing of inspirations—in this case, those of its four owners: Randy Moon, LCD Soundsystem's James Murphy, Christina Topsøe, and wine director Justin Chearno. Not quite a wine bar, not quite a restaurant, it defies easy classification. It's Danish *hygge* plus the loose elegance of Paris. It's Scandinavian design paired with Japanese compactness. With cozy touches and well-loved artifacts, it's also a little bit DIY. It succeeds in feeling like that neighborhood spot where you want to linger. In a city like New York, with its cramped apartments, tiny kitchens, and canceled trains, isn't that what everyone's looking for? The excuse to stay a little longer—just one more glass, please.

CEREAL: How were you introduced to natural wine?

RANDY MOON: It was the raucous natural-wine-bar environment that got me before the wine did. When I lived in Sydney, one of my regular spots was a bottle shop and bar called 121BC, named after the first historical reference to a good wine vintage. When it was too busy on the bar side, we just sat on the floor in the cold room while a seemingly endless line of friends came in to grab a bottle, chat, snack, and pore through the almost all-Italian hit list. I get the same feeling at Ahiru Store in Tokyo, Brawn in London, and all the other great natural wine bars and restaurants around the world. I just want to stay all night.

JUSTIN CHEARNO: In 2002 I was working in a Williamsburg wine shop. The buyer there became obsessed with some of the earliest natural wines coming to the United States. They completely changed my idea of what wine could or should be. I didn't necessarily like the wines at first—many were flawed—but they were still compelling and they felt worth paying attention to in a way that conventional wines didn't. It was also the first time I had such a direct connection to the winemaker. That in itself was mind-blowing. New York is now one of the greatest wine-drinking cities in the world due to our amazing access to older classic wines.

CEREAL: What are some of your favorite memories from your time at The Four Horsemen?

RM: We've had a great time figuring out what makes a restaurant work in Brooklyn, and which of our pipe dreams are accomplishable—such as our guest chef series we call The Fifth Horseman, where Stephen Harris of The Sportsman and Thomas Keller came to cook.

CEREAL: The wine comes from all over the world. How do you create a workable context for the NYC customer?

RM: We don't make a fuss about it, but we really are a super-local business. We get our produce from nearby, our GM and chef have both lived in Brooklyn for more than ten years, and all four of us live a stone's throw away. James and Justin have been in Williamsburg since the 1990s—they tell me you had to take the L train back to the East Village to find an ATM in those days. The point is, when guests come to the restaurant, they also come to our neighborhood.

CEREAL: What inspired the setting?

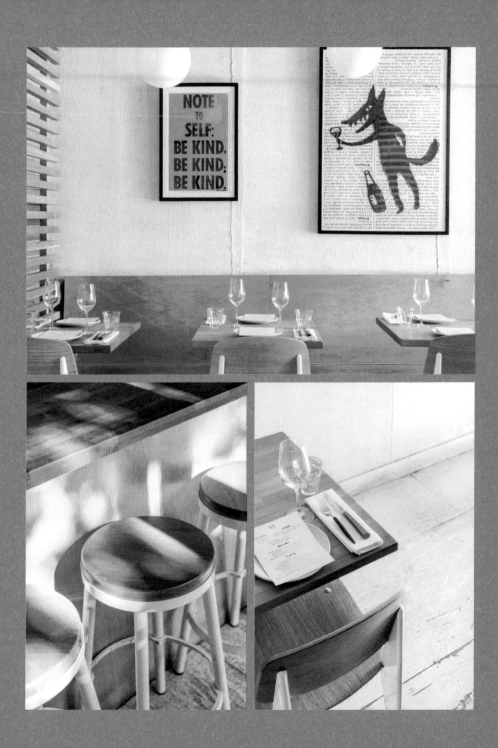

RM: Everything—design, food, wine, music, service—was conceived entirely as a self-serving attempt to create a place we felt didn't quite exist in New York, and which the four of us and our friends wanted to go to. We travel a lot, and our favorite places to eat and drink in Tokyo, London, Paris, and Copenhagen have also been highly influential. We wanted a place that surprised guests by feeling casual and unassuming yet at the same time delivered food, wine, and an overall dining experience to a very high standard. A place you can walk into for a quick glass of wine and end up lingering for hours. The space is small, but we had high ambitions for the food being produced in the kitchen and the number of people we wanted to accommodate in the restaurant. We also wanted an actual bar toward the front of the room. Fitting it all in was a bit like playing *Tetris*. We took a lot of inspiration from Japan, where spaces are often tiny yet still feel interesting and not claustrophobic. Every square inch is used, including storage under the banquettes and high up on the walls right next to the ceiling. In response to the dark, reclaimed aesthetic that dominated Brooklyn restaurants, we decided early on that it had to feel light, with gentle textures, lots of white, and natural materials; part Copenhagen, part Japan. We play only full-length albums—it was important to us that the acoustics were generous, making it possible to hear the people you're having dinner with, but not the ones sitting two tables over. James used his experience building recording studios to adjust the acoustics; sound is diffused and absorbed in a way that works for the space.

JC: Le Verre Volé in Paris, 10 William St. in Sydney, and many others were reference points for us. We used a lot of economical materials—plywood on the floor, cedar for the ceiling slats, burlap on the walls. Teak was our only luxury. The wine shelving in our cellar was repurposed from the wine shop that Justin managed for years. We had a banquette on only one side of the dining room when we opened, but when *Master of None* shot an episode here, they mirrored the banquette on the other side of the room and put up a decorative cedar slat wall. It looked so good we kept it!

———

FOURHORSEMENBK.COM

MY NEW YORK

by KAI AVENT-DELEON OF SINCERELY, TOMMY

photos by CERRUTI DRAIME

Founder of Sincerely, Tommy, Kai is a home-grown New Yorker who was inspired to create a place that could unify her beloved community of Bed-Stuy. Her shop consists of an eclectic mix of fashion, jewelery and art, a hive in which the new residents and natives come to connect.

My shop, Sincerely, Tommy, is a concept boutique that sells the work of emerging global artists and designers. It is located just a few blocks from where I grew up in Bed-Stuy, Brooklyn. Creating a space for open dialogue, creative discovery, and conversation to connect the community is at the heart of what I do.

I grew up in a household with two creative, activist, New York City–native parents, who exposed me to a lot from a very young age. I was a weird kid, curious about everything and often drawn to things that weren't popular.

Growing up in New York, I was surrounded by a beautiful mix of influences—it's unlike anywhere else. Anything you are interested in is available for you to learn about, try, or discover. I went to a performing arts high school, where I studied drama, photography, dance, and music. I started taking summer classes at the Fashion Institute of Technology when I was still in high school to learn about fashion. Looking back, I realize my style and specific aesthetic come from pairing together different parts of all these influences; street style with costumes from the plays I was in, high fashion and technical fits, the women I met and observed.

See page 98 for information on Sincerely, Tommy

I never intended to work for someone else; it's not in my nature. Opening a store has always been a dream of mine. My mother and grandmother were pioneers. They started businesses of their own in Bed-Stuy at a time and place when that wasn't the norm. All they wanted to do was work in order to create the neighborhood they wanted to exist. It set the tone for me to be brave and daring—making up the rules as you go along was my example. There were so many newer residents moving to Bed-Stuy from the city, including artists, creatives, and young people, and I wanted to figure out a way to speak to both them and the older residents who had lived there for decades. I wasn't trying to start a movement. It was my vision to inspire other creatives—particularly women of color—to cultivate their visions, dreams, and art into something we could all relate to, with a space that was created specifically for the community.

Bed-Stuy is a changing area, and it is such a reflection of Brooklyn as a whole. It is a place for so many different voices. And it is my home. My concern and desire to connect with those who have been here for years grows as I see the neighborhood change.

I think the most memorable and meaningful conversation I've ever had was at an event we hosted, focused on bridging the gap between natives of Bed-Stuy and new residents. It was beautiful to hear the stories of the people who had moved here decades ago, and have stayed because they love the energy of this neighborhood. We also talked with newer residents about why younger generations are attracted here. It was fascinating! It's a never-ending dialogue that shows more than just a cycle of gentrification—it tells the story of change in general.

Originally, I thought my next step would be to open a second store in order to grow the brand. But I'm realizing that what I really want to do is go deeper into what already exists here. As the world grows into a space where we are pushed away from organic connections, and our lives are lived more digitally, I want to continue moving in a direction that promotes the opposite.

My new passion project, Sanctuary (A Healing Space for Women), is just one of the programs I created to allow women to share their stories in an intimate and vulnerable way. Every time we gather, I am reminded that these kinds of spaces are crucial.

My store is a canvas for creativity, and as I continue exploring who I am, what my passions are, and what I am drawn to, the space will remain a place for me to express that in whatever form it takes. I feel as though the people who can relate to that process are usually the ones who end up being drawn to hang out here.

———

SINCERELYTOMMY.COM

MY NEW YORK

by LINDA RODIN

*Linda Rodin's infatuation with New York has kept her rooted
in the city for over five decades. Stimulating an insatiable
appetite for fashion, beauty, and life, her life as a model, stylist,
and as the founder of RODIN olio lusso was nurtured by this
great metropolis.*

I grew up thirty minutes away from Manhattan, so coming here
wasn't this grand excursion. It wasn't like I got off a train from
Chicago and ended up in the Big City. I was always in the Big
City for school trips, and for museums. I went to Italy for a few
years when I was eighteen, but I came back. I officially moved to
New York City in 1967. I could still go home and do laundry at my
parents' house. My sister and I would take our dirty clothes on the
train. It was never a big move—let's put it that way.

My first apartment was on the Upper West Side. I shared it with a
friend. We painted it purple and it was very of-the-moment, very
late-sixties. I worked in an art gallery. That was one of my first jobs.
It was new art, modern art, not Picassos and things. I remember
just loving being in that atmosphere. The gallery was in a loft in
Soho, an area nobody knew about at the time. It was like being in
new territory, and it was wonderful.

Some time after that, I decided that I wanted to be a fashion
photographer. My sister, at one point, said to me, "You know, you
don't take great pictures, but you do get great clothes. Maybe that's
a job." I said, "What kind of job would that be?" We had never
heard the word "stylist" before. We didn't know what that word
even meant.

One thing led to another, as it always does. I worked for a fashion
photographer before I opened my own boutique in Soho. It was
called Linda Hopp. I designed clothes. I bought Todd Oldham
and early Calvin Klein. It was all very exciting, but it didn't last
long. After that I decided to see if I could be a "stylist"—whatever
that meant. It was all just by default. I've been in fashion without
knowing it for a very long time.

The industry has changed since I first started, and so has New York. Every corner is a Duane Reade or a bank. I go away for a week and when I come back, there's another condo. There isn't a shoemaker left in the city. There are no drugstores anymore. We used to have the most fabulous drugstores. The city is so different, and I miss the way it was. But there's no place like home, and I'm still here—even though I don't love it the way I used to.

You have to make your peace with wherever you are. I spend a lot of time in my apartment. I found it forty years ago. I had broken up with my boyfriend at the time and had to find a spot quickly. It was one of those things. I found a place in Chelsea, on Fifteenth Street, which was not a neighborhood you wanted to live in. The first apartment I had was a tiny studio I rented for 400 dollars a month. Later, I moved within the building to where I am now. For a long time, before all the new buildings went up, I could see all of Lower Manhattan to the south and the Empire State Building to the north. I had a view of the Hudson River. On any given day, I could see sailboats and cruise ships. It was just heaven on earth.

I was lucky. I was in my twenties, and I was here, in a New York City that was still New York City, and it was fantastic. You didn't have to say, "I made it here." You just lived, and that was enough. We took it for granted. It was our town. This place has afforded me my life, and who I am. I've met fascinating people, done interesting things. I've never even thought about living anywhere else, have never considered leaving my apartment. Anyway, once you're a New Yorker, you're a New Yorker. It gets in your blood.

LINCOLN CENTER

words by LUCY BROOK
photos by MATTHEW JOHNSON

It was summer 2011 when I first clapped eyes on Lincoln Center. The city was a hot labyrinth of asphalt and tinfoil skyscrapers glinting in the afternoon sun, and I was a tourist, wide-eyed and awestruck by my first visit to a place I'd only ever seen on celluloid. I'd been whisked from JFK's heaving heart to the Hotel Beacon on the leafy Upper West Side, where the streets were wide and, as I realized when I moved to the East Village eighteen months later, comparatively clean. I asked the driver if I could sit up front so I could see the city, and he agreed, pointing out landmarks along the way: "There's the UN; Times Square is thataway." He told me in his thick New Jersey accent, when we pulled up, that riding in the front was, "you know, kind of a faux pas." I dropped my bags and hit the streets, sultry and humming in the early evening, quickly losing any sense of direction. I confused Broadway for Columbus Avenue and ended up right in front of it. Lincoln Center, with its monumental entrance, majestic arches, and dancing fountain, felt instantly familiar, a quintessential New York landmark, looming in the summer twilight. Not wanting to stray too far from the hotel, I wandered around the iconic main plaza before finding a spot by the fountain, where I watched guests arrive in suits and cocktail dresses for a performance at the Metropolitan Opera House.

Lincoln Center is so enmeshed with the cultural fabric of New York City that it's difficult to imagine it was conceived and built in only the 1950s and 1960s. Today, it forms a 16.3-acre slice of culture, and a beloved hub for the arts, attracting five million visitors each year and known across the globe for its world-class facilities and performances. Spanning from Sixty-Second Street to the south, to

Sixty-Sixth Street to the north, and bordered by Amsterdam and Columbus Avenues, Lincoln Center comprises thirty indoor and outdoor performance venues, including the Metropolitan Opera House, Avery Fisher Hall, where the New York Philharmonic orchestra makes its classical magic, and the David H. Koch Theater, New York City Ballet's home stage. Lincoln Center houses eleven resident arts organizations, from the opera, ballet, and orchestra to the revered Juilliard School, one of the world's leading performing arts institutions.

Following a radical redesign in the early 2000s that altered not just the physical appearance of Lincoln Center but also the public's perception of it, the venue has evolved from a conservative bastion of the Upper West Side into a thoroughly modern facility that democratizes the arts. Playing host to countless public festivals and free concerts, it also houses exclusive events.

The development of Lincoln Center for the Performing Arts was spurred on by John D. Rockefeller III, who raised more than half of the 184.5 million dollars required to bring it into existence as part of the Lincoln Square Renewal Project in the 1950s. The idea—to create an island for the arts in New York and unite the city's cultural institutions, then dotted around Manhattan—was, at the time, an outlandish one. The United States had never seen a performing arts center, and, as well as having to define why Lincoln Center would be beneficial for the city, campaigners often had to explain what a performing arts center actually was. The Upper West Side wasn't yet the stately neighborhood it is today, and some detractors fretted over moving the city's respected cultural organizations to an area regularly blighted by crime. Urban renewal finally succeeded, and Lincoln Center's completion between 1962 and 1966 heralded change for the Upper West Side, affirming New York as a bona fide cultural capital. By the 1990s, however, Lincoln Center had lost a little of its luster and was seen as a remote and somewhat intimidating arts facility, accessible only to society's upper echelons. In a city forever in flux, Lincoln Center needed to evolve into a contemporary, user-friendly cultural destination, without losing the design elements that had made it a landmark.

"The question really was how to make this place more inviting, more connected, more successful—less a kind of travertine mausoleum to culture, and more a part of the ongoing functioning city," said Pulitzer Prize–winning architecture critic Paul Goldberger of Lincoln Center in 2011. Diller Scofidio + Renfro, an architecture firm better known for its art installations than its buildings, brought a maverick spirit to the 2006 1.2-billion-dollar redevelopment, hurtling Lincoln Center and its venues into the twenty-first century without stripping them of their character. The new pedestrian promenade and Hypar Pavilion lawn and restaurant were rapturously received, as was the extensive redesign of Alice Tully Hall, the expansion of the School of American Ballet, and the addition of public spaces throughout the campus. Since my move to New York in 2012, I've become a regular at Lincoln Center, falling head over heels for the breadth of its cultural offerings. I've seen Shakespeare's magnificent tragedy *Macbeth* brought to life by Lincoln Center Theater, and had my senses tickled by the vibrant Gorillaz opera, *Monkey: Journey to the West*, as part of the ever-imaginative Lincoln Center Festival. I've watched with wonder as the chandeliers were raised in the Metropolitan Opera House, all plush red velvet and twinkling gold ceilings, and, like the rest of the audience, left misty-eyed after a devastatingly beautiful performance of *Madama Butterfly*. Last December, I watched the New York City Ballet dance *The Nutcracker* at the David H. Koch Theater, where the sugarplum fairy elicited squeals of glee from the children next to me, and theater magic made it snow indoors until the entire stage resembled a giant snow globe. Outside, the year's first real snow was falling, blanketing the plaza in powdery white. The children, delighted that art had become life, threw soft snowballs at one another as the feathery flakes stuck to their hair. The fountain danced on.

LINCOLNCENTER.ORG

101 SPRING STREET

words by JOHN PAWSON
photos by JUSTIN CHUNG

I spent a great deal of time placing the art and a great deal designing the renovation in accordance. Everything from the first was intended to be thoroughly considered and to be permanent.

—Donald Judd, 1989

Like no one else, Judd understood the significance of space. In place of the term "minimalism," he preferred to speak of the simple expression of complex thought, and 101 Spring Street—like Marfa—is a perfect embodiment of this demanding manifesto. In a nineteenth-century, cast-iron corner building, arranged over five stories above two basements, Judd shows that space does not have to be crafted from scratch to feel special and refined. Everywhere you move, you are conscious of being in space that is comfortable, for people and for art. Because the found conditions were different on each level of the building, each intervention is also slightly different. On the top floor, for example, he used the same oak for the baseboards as for the floor, so that the floor reads as a recessed plane. On the third floor, in contrast, he chose to have no baseboards at all, instead running a gap between the walls and the floor, which quietly but completely changes the spatial composition. There is a special, intimate charge to the atmosphere because Judd has created the perfect circumstances for installing art—his own and other people's—in an environment that is also, unequivocally, a home. This is a place for living, working, and gathering, from the utensils in the industrial kitchen, the platform bed, and the standing desk, down to the hinged timber flap that his two children, Rainer and Flavin, used as a play theater. I remember visiting Luis Barragán's house in Mexico City some years ago and having a powerful sense of the man having just left the room. In Spring Street the feeling is even more overwhelming, not least because I met Judd and have a clear memory of what his presence meant in a place.

JUDDFOUNDATION.ORG

ADDITIONAL INFORMATION

ARCHITECTURE

POINTS OF INTEREST

1 FLATIRON BUILDING

D.H. Burnham & Co., *1902*. 175 5th Avenue, New York, NY 10010.

2 SEAGRAM BUILDING

Ludwig Mies van der Rohe and Philip Johnson, *1958*. 375 Park Avenue, New York, NY 10152.

3 OCULUS

Santiago Calatrava, *2016*. WTC Transportation Hub, New York, NY 10007.

4 THE MET BREUER

Marcel Breuer, *1966*. 945 Madison Avenue, New York, NY 10021.

5 41 COOPER SQUARE

Thom Mayne of Morphosis, *2009*. 41 Cooper Square, New York, NY 10008.

6 HIGH LINE PARK

James Corner Field Operations, *2009*. New York, NY 10011.

7 GRAND CENTRAL TERMINAL

Reed and Stem & Warren and Wetmore, *1913*. 89 East 42nd Street, New York, NY 10017.

8 NEW MUSEUM

SANAA, *2007*. 253 Bowery, New York, NY 10002.

ART

POINTS OF INTEREST

1 WHITNEY MUSEUM OF AMERICAN ART

Museum, 99 Gansevoort Street, New York, NY 10014.

2 MUSEUM OF MODERN ART

Museum, 11 West 53rd Street, New York, NY 10019.

3 MATTHEW MARKS

Gallery, 523 West 24th Street, New York, NY 10011.

4 PACE

Gallery, 510 West 25th Street, New York, NY 10001.

5 NEUE GALERIE NEW YORK

Museum, 1048 5th Avenue, New York, NY 10028.

6 DAVID ZWIRNER

Gallery, 525 West 19th Street, New York, NY 10011.

7 THE METROPOLITAN MUSEUM OF ART

Museum, 1000 5th Avenue, New York, NY 10028.

8 SOLOMON R. GUGGENHEIM MUSEUM

Museum, 1071 5th Avenue, New York, NY 10128.

9 THE NOGUCHI MUSEUM

Museum, 9-01 33rd Road, Long Island City, NY 11106.

10 THE MORGAN LIBRARY & MUSEUM

Library & Museum, 225 Madison Avenue,
New York, NY 10016.

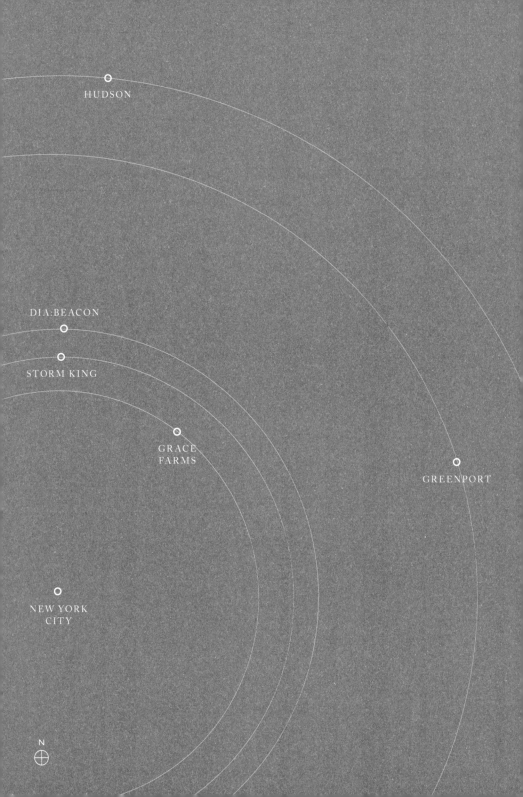

HUDSON

DIA:BEACON

STORM KING

GRACE
FARMS

GREENPORT

NEW YORK
CITY

N

WEEKEND TRIPS

54 miles (87 km)   **GRACE FARMS**
90 minutes by car.

For a serene wander under the winding River Building by SANAA, cradled within pristine countryside.

60 miles (97 km)   **STORM KING**
90 minutes by car.

For 500 acres (200 hectares) of contemporary outdoor sculptures, founded in 1960 by Ralph E. Ogden.

66 miles (106 km)   **DIA:BEACON**
90 minutes by train, or 1 hour and 45 minutes by car.

For the vast contemporary art gallery, redeveloped from a 1929 factory by the collaboration of Dia Art Foundation and Robert Irwin, who also designed the surrounding garden.

100 miles (161 km)   **GREENPORT**
2 hours and 50 minutes by train, or 2 hours and 30 minutes by car.

For a laid-back coastal break, made extra special with a stay at American Beech, and the possibility of taking the ferry to Shelter Island for the day.

120 miles (193 km)   **HUDSON**
2 hours by train, or 2 hours and 30 minutes by car.

For the thriving food scene as well as antiquing. A stay or a meal at The Maker, conveniently located on the main street in town (Warren Street), is a must.

1   BAGEL FROM RUSS & DAUGHTERS

One of the oldest delis in New York, it has been catering for
the locals of the Lower East Side since 1914. Wire baskets
of plump pumpernickel and *shissel* rye hang beside rows of
preserves, all behind a glass counter loaded with deep pink
smoked fish. Their soft, golden bagels are an institution
in themselves.

2   HONEY DIP DOUGHNUT FROM PETER PAN DONUT
    & PASTRY SHOP

Enclosed behind a mint-green exterior is a Neverland of
doughnut delights. Across checkered floors and white counters,
rows of baked goods await keen consumers who line up through
the door to devour them. Flavors range from red velvet to
coconut-encrusted white cream to French toast, but the honey
dip doughnut is a classic. Its sugary, sumptuous simplicity
cannot be beaten. Purchase at least half a dozen—eating them
all in one sitting is optional.

3   THE MILK BAR SAMPLER FROM MILK BAR

Christina Tosi's beloved Milk Bar empire is celebrated for
its rainbow-sprinkled three-layer cakes, soft cookies, and
delicious pies. If, like us, you have no hope choosing between
their delectable treats, opt for the Milk Bar Sampler – a tin tray
containing a taste of everything: a slice of gooey Milk Bar Pie,
six 'B'day' cake truffles, and one of every variety of cookie on
offer. With ten stores strewn across New York, there really is no
excuse not to drop by and satiate your sugar cravings.

4   OLIVE OIL FROM ORACLE

Named for the ancient oracle at Delphi, and with a figurative logo inspired by Cycladic sculpture, everything about Oracle's olive oil is rooted in the ancient traditions of Greece. Their small-batch extra virgin oil is made from Koroneiki olives, sourced from a collective of sustainable farms on the coast of Laconia, and picked for their balanced flavor, low acidity, and anti-inflammatory properties. Keep a bottle to hand in your kitchen to elevate any meal.

5   HANDMADE SOAP FROM SAIPUA

Saipua is a multi-disciplinary collective with flower arranging and soap-making at its heart. The group moved upstate to Montgomery County to establish Worlds End Farm, where they now grow their own flowers, graze a herd of Icelandic sheep, and host artist residencies. Their soaps are made on site and by hand using olive oil and shea butter, fragranced with essential oils such as cedar wood, lavender, and patchouli. For a day out of the city, book an appointment to visit the experimental 107-acre farm.

A DAY IN NEW YORK

9 A.M.   **LA MERCERIE**

Start your day the right way with a crispy, grilled Crêpe Complète, filled with a sunny-side-up egg, ham, and 18-month matured Comté cheese. Wash it down with a drip coffee or specialty tea. Alternatively, if you are in a rush, grab a croissant to go from the pastry counter. *See page 50*

11 A.M.   **LA GARÇONNE**

Swing by La Garçonne, a spacious, white-walled boutique in Tribeca, for the finest in luxurious yet understated womenswear, as well as a small selection of homewares. See page 106

NOON   **DASHWOOD BOOKS**

Wander over to Dashwood to peruse their selection of photography books. With a specialist collection of rare and out-of-print tomes, you are bound to encounter a surprising discovery on the shelves. *See page 134*

1:30 P.M.   **EN JAPANESE BRASSERIE**

Have a modern Japanese meal at EN. Order the freshly made scooped tofu. We prefer it served warm, drenched in *wari joyu*. *See page 78*

3 P.M. TÉ COMPANY

Just a ten-minute stroll from EN, Té Company is the ideal place to enjoy a cup of tea. They specialize in Taiwanese tea and sell loose-leaf varieties alongside beautiful wares, including porcelain *gaiwan*. *See page 46*

4:30 P.M. THE MORGAN LIBRARY & MUSEUM

Hop in a taxi and make your way toward Midtown to The Morgan Library & Museum. Explore J.P. Morgan's 1906 library, filled with rare books and manuscripts. *See page 138*

6 P.M. BEMELMANS BAR AT THE CARLYLE

For a taste of Art Deco New York, stop by Bemelmans Bar at The Carlyle for an aperitif. *See page 42*

8 P.M. FLORA BAR

Dine at Flora Bar for your last meal of the day. Housed in an open space on the lower level of The Met Breuer, this restaurant has an inventive menu that revolves around seafood. *See page 90*

CEREAL PACKING TIPS

OUR SIX ESSENTIALS

TOTE BAG

A lightweight, foldable tote bag is handy when you buy one too many souvenirs and can't fit them all in your suitcase. It's also a great option for carrying your daily essentials as you explore the city.

SUPPLEMENTS

A small pillbox of supplements such as echinacea, vitamins, and Korean ginseng can prove useful when on the road. Jet lag and changes in temperature and environment can make you feel run-down. It's a good idea to give your immune system a boost!

SCARF

A large scarf will not only keep you warm when it's cold and protect you from the sun when it's hot; it will also double as a much-needed blanket on flights and train journeys. Choose the material of your scarf according to your destination: linen for warmer climes, and wool or cashmere for chillier weather.

BUTTON-DOWN SHIRT

A white button-down shirt is the ultimate staple for any travel wardrobe. Pick a fit and style that work for you then dress it up or dress it down according to the occasion. And it goes with almost everything, which allows you to pack light. Pair it with trousers or jeans for daytime meetings, transition into evening by adding a blazer, or throw it over a swimsuit for poolside lounging.

MUSIC

Download the Cereal Spotify playlist before you leave! It's the perfect companion for those long-haul flights, train rides, and road trips.

readcereal.com/playlist

ESSENTIAL OIL

An essential oil in your scent of choice is a must. Depending on the oil, it can be used as a moisturizer, facial cleanser, makeup remover, beard oil, bug repellent, and calming meditative ointment.

ABOUT THE EDITORS

Rosa Park is cofounder and editor in chief of
Cereal. Rich Stapleton is Cereal's cofounder
and creative director. They travel extensively
for the magazine and were inspired to create
a series of city guides that highlighted their
favorite places to visit. Cereal is a biannual
magazine known for its original take on design,
style, and travel.

readcereal.com